Contents

KW-054-427

1 Introduction

What kinds of transport have you used in the last seven days? Make a list. Travelling quickly and comfortably from place to place is something we take for granted, but not so long ago the only way most people could get around was on foot. How we travel, and the speed at which we do so, is changing rapidly. When your grandparents were young, only very rich people could afford to travel by air, and the hovercraft and jet engine had not yet been invented. The bicycles, cars and planes of today will soon become out-of-date and historical relics.

People's lives have been completely changed by improvements in transport. By studying these improvements we can get a better understanding of the world as it was, and as it is today. This book will show you how to explore your neighbourhood and other areas to discover

A horse-drawn bus, as used at the beginning of this century. Public transport, like every other form of transport, has changed a great deal in the last eighty years or so. Compare this picture with the picture at the top of page 5.

EXPLORING
TRANSPORT

Cliff Lines

Illustrated by Stephen Wheele

Wayland

Exploring the Past

Exploring Buildings

Exploring Clothes

Exploring Communications

Exploring Farming

Exploring Industry

Exploring People

Exploring Schools

Exploring Shopping

Exploring Sport and Recreation

Exploring Transport

Series Editor: Stephen Setford
Designed by: David Armitage

Cover picture: A busy London traffic scene, 1921.

First published in 1988 by
Wayland (Publishers) Ltd
61 Western Road, Hove
East Sussex, England BN3 1JD

British Library Cataloguing in Publication Data
Lines, C.J.
    Exploring transport. – (Exploring the past).
    1. Transportation – History
    I. Title   HE151
    380.5′09

    ISBN 0–85210–003–6

Phototypeset by Kalligraphics Ltd, Redhill, Surrey
Printed in Italy by G. Canale & C.S.p.A., Turin
Bound in the U.K. by The Bath Press, Avon

Many people in Britain rely entirely on public transport to get from place to place. There are more than 70,000 buses in Britain, many of them double-deckers, like those in the picture.

evidence of transport in the past. All the clues you need are in the pages that follow and – if you follow them carefully – they will help you to unravel the fascinating history of transport.

Travelling around

How do you travel to school? The diagram below shows how pupils in a class in Reading travel to school and the distances they cover. The school is near several new housing estates, where most

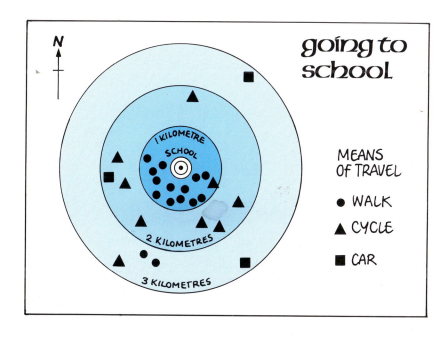

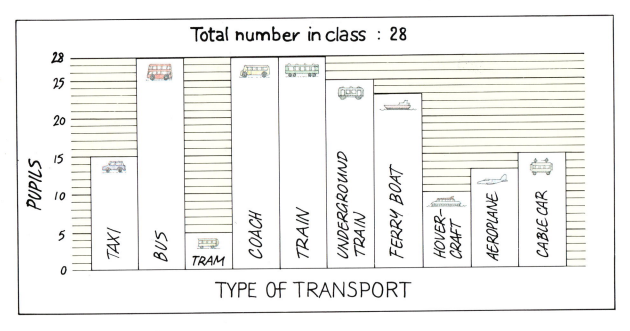

Total number in class : 28

PUPILS

28
25
20
15
10
5
0

TAXI   BUS   TRAM   COACH   TRAIN   UNDERGROUND TRAIN   FERRY BOAT   HOVER-CRAFT   AEROPLANE   CABLE CAR

TYPE OF TRANSPORT

of the pupils live. There are many more forms of transport today than there were in the past. The bar chart above shows the different forms of public transport another class of eleven-year-olds have used at some time or another. What other forms of public transport have you used that do not appear on the chart? The pupils did not include such things as escalators and lifts, which transport us over short distances.

Passengers leaving an Inter City 125 high-speed train at London's King's Cross Station. How many places connected with public transport are there in your area or town?

A surprising amount of the land around us is used for transport purposes, so that we can travel to places quickly and comfortably. For example, walking down the street would be very unpleasant without a proper pavement, and shopping is made much easier if there is a large car park nearby. In towns and cities much land is taken up by transport centres such as coach and railway stations, taxi cab ranks and bus depots. There are also travel agencies, petrol stations and bicycle shops, each providing a service for travellers.

Make two charts like those on pages 5 and 6 using surveys of your class. You will need a copy of a map, showing the roads around your school, to help you make the circular diagram.

Make a list of places in your town or district connected with public transport and mark them on a local map. Mark also the main routes of buses, trains and so on. Do you notice any pattern in the way public transport services are distributed? Are some areas served better or worse than others? Can you think of any reasons for this?

Above *A multi-storey car park; just one example of how land in our towns and cities is used for transport purposes.*

Below *A busy traffic scene in London's Oxford Street.*

2 Air Transport

More than fifty million people use British airports each year and one fifth of the goods we sell and buy abroad travel by air. In some areas of the British Isles, such as the Orkney Islands, air travel is essential to the well-being of the community. Package tours, in which flights and accommodation are arranged by tour operators have made it possible for many people to take their annual holiday overseas. Although expensive, it is even possible to fly from London to New York and back in a day on Concorde.

Aircraft and air travel have developed very rapidly since the first transatlantic flight by Alcock and Brown in 1919. In the same year a British company started passenger flights from London to Paris. By 1939 the main British airline, Imperial Airways, operated a network of flights to different parts of the world, and airports had been built close to many British cities.

Two pictures which show how much aircraft have developed in just seventy years. **Below left** *Soldiers in Northern Ireland guard the crashed aircraft of Alcock and Brown after their transatlantic flight in 1919.* **Below right** *The supersonic passenger aeroplane* Concorde *in flight.*

what to look for

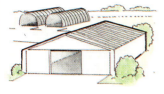
Hangars and sections of concrete runway in areas of fairly level land.

Memorials and written relics, often connected with the 1914-18 or 1939-45 wars.

Aircraft or parts of aircraft in Museums and displays.

Pub names and signs near old airfields and places where aircraft were built.

Left *Some items to look out for connected with air travel in your area.*

Find Croydon on a map of London. London's main airport used to be at Croydon. After the Second World War (1939-1945), it proved to be too small for the newer, larger aircraft that were being built and increasing passenger traffic. It closed in 1957, but the control tower, hotel and parts of the airfield can still be seen. What are the main airports serving London today?

During the Second World War, airfields were hastily built in many parts of the country. After the war the land became farmland once more but concrete runways, hangars and other buildings can still be seen. Only a few wartime airfields, like Biggin Hill in Kent, are in use today.

The chart above gives you clues on what to look for in connection with air transport in your district. Design an inn sign and suggest a name for a pub near a busy airport.

3 Travelling by road

When did your parents or other adults you know buy their first car? Motor cars first appeared on the roads in the 1890s but for many years only very rich people could afford them. A few of these early cars, known as 'veterans', can still be seen and every November some take part in the London to Brighton Veteran Car Run. Cars gradually became more common but it is only since about 1960 that the number of people owning cars has increased very rapidly. There are over twice as many cars on the roads today as there were in 1964. As a result, fewer people use buses and trains, and bicycle sales have dropped. In 1987 there were over 17 million vehicles on the roads in Britain – nearly one for every three members of the population.

Veteran cars are often exhibited at shows and rallies. The London to Brighton annual Veteran Car Run is a particularly good chance to see what the cars of the past looked like.

The interchange of the M4 and M5 motorways near Bristol. The transport revolution of the twentieth century has changed the appearance of much of our countryside.

Below *A guide to identifying the age of a car from its registration number. Registration numbers on cars built before 1963 are an unreliable way of finding how old a car is.*

How old is that car?	
Letter at end of registration e.g. RNO 371D	
A 1963	
B 1964	
C 1965	
D 1966	
E 1967	
Registration moved from 1 January to 1 August	
F 1968	P 1975/76
G 1968/69	R 1976/77
H 1969/70	S 1977/78
J 1970/71	T 1978/79
K 1971/72	V 1979/80
L 1972/73	W 1980/81
M 1973/74	X 1981/82
N 1974/75	Y 1982/83
Letter at beginning of registration e.g. C505 THC	
A 1983/84	
B 1984/85	
C 1985/86	
D 1986/87	
E 1987/88	

Fifty years ago most goods were carried by train; today they go by road. In the 1930s trucks were small and not very powerful. Improvements in engineering and design have made them larger, more powerful, and able to carry all kinds of goods from frozen foods to furniture.

Roads have had to be improved and new ones built to cope with the increase in traffic. We are in the middle of a 'transport revolution' with motor vehicles helping to change our way of life and altering the appearance of the countryside, as well as our towns and cities.

Cars and trucks have a limited life and most end up as scrap metal, so that early models are more likely to be seen in museums and in the pages of old magazines than on the roads. However, there are many old people who can tell you what it was like driving cars in the days before electric starter-motors and motorways. Use the chart opposite to help you make a survey of the age of vehicles passing your home or school.

The Changing Road

Are there any major roadworks or new roads being built in your district? Roads are constantly being altered, new junctions made and road signs changed, so that we soon forget what the roads once looked like. Photographs taken only fifty years ago show roads without traffic islands, pedestrian crossings, cat's-eyes and other features which we take for granted today. One hundred years ago most main roads were made of layers of stone chips; they were known as macadamed roads, after the Scottish engineer John McAdam who designed them. Find out how a macadamed road was constructed and what materials were used. Why were they an improvement on previous methods of road building?

When cars and trucks began to appear, more improvements had to be made. To stop the stones flying, roads were given a surface of tar and later they were tarmacadamed (covered with stone

Above *A section of motorway under construction in Devon.*

A Member of Parliament, Sir John Dickson-Poynder, sits proudly in his new car in 1897.

chips coated with tar). Speed limits were introduced at the same time, to save the roads from being broken up and to save money. These were as low as 20 mph (32 kph) until 1930.

The first major road improvements started in the 1950s. The amount of traffic began to grow rapidly and delays, accidents and congestion showed that the road system could not cope with the increasing traffic. The motorway network was the first attempt to build long-distance roads specifically for motor traffic. New by-passes, bridges, fly-overs, tunnels and ring roads have also been built. The old roads have been widened, straightened and provided with roundabouts and other safety features.

Old photographs of your district will show you what the roads used to be like. Compare one of these photographs with the same spot today. Make sketches to show the road as it was, and as it is now. Discuss any changes made.

An outing in a charabanc, Torquay, 1926. Until 1930, speed limits were as low as 20 mph (32 kph). This postcard was written by the boy sitting in the back seat with his parents.

4 Railway closures

When more people and goods began to travel by road, the railways started to lose money. In 1963 it was decided to close many branch lines, especially those in country areas which never made a profit. A few stretches of line were bought by groups of people who wanted to preserve them and run steam trains once more. Some of these railways, such as the Keighley and Worth Valley Light Railway in Yorkshire, run regular services which are very popular with visitors.

The branch lines which were closed have not vanished completely and there are many relics to be seen along the routes they once took. These routes can be found on the 1: 50,000 Ordnance Survey maps, where the line is shown with its cuttings and embankments and labelled 'Course of old railway'. Most of the equipment (such as signals and track) has gone, but many of the buildings, bridges and tunnels can still be seen.

Above *Steam locomotives rusting away at a scrapyard in South Wales.*

A steam train leaves Howarth for Keighley, on Yorkshire's Keighley and Worth Valley Light Railway. There are quite a number of small private lines, run by steam enthusiasts who want to preserve steam trains for the public to enjoy.

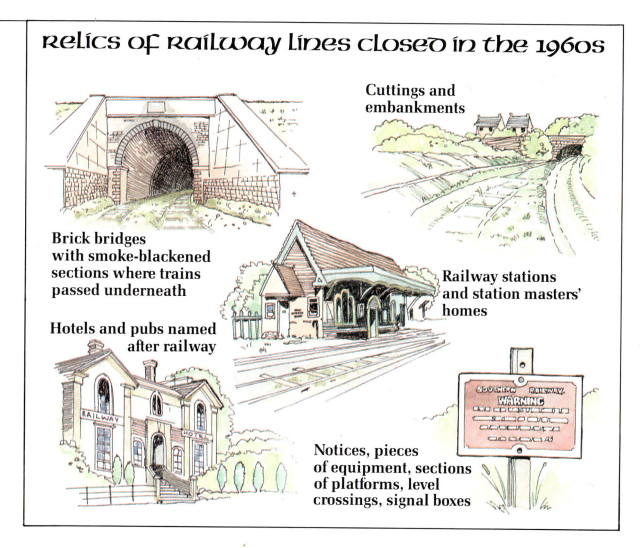

Relics of railway lines closed in the 1960s

Cuttings and embankments

Brick bridges with smoke-blackened sections where trains passed underneath

Railway stations and station masters' homes

Hotels and pubs named after railway

Notices, pieces of equipment, sections of platforms, level crossings, signal boxes

The Cuckoo Line

One line which closed in 1968 ran from Tunbridge Wells in Kent to the south coast. It was called the Cuckoo Line because in Spring passengers could hear cuckoos calling in the woods near the line. The chart below shows how one station on the line lost its importance. Make a picture graph to illustrate the decrease in importance of Hailsham station as shown by the chart.

Hailsham station	1924	1957	1967
Passenger tickets sold	89,000	67,000	48,000
Number of goods trains each week	15	3	1
Goods sent from station (tonnes)	1,900	500	30
Coal unloaded at station (tonnes)	5,500	4,300	3,300

5 Travel in the twenties

When your grandparents were very young their families probably could not afford to run a car. Cars were still luxuries and most people used buses, trams or trains. Bicycles were popular and many small goods such as bread were delivered on what was called a tradesman's bike, which had a wide basket fixed over the front wheel. Ice-cream sellers had large tricycles with containers in front of them to carry the ice-creams. Heavy goods, such as coal, were carried by horse-drawn carts, which slowed up the traffic in busy streets. Street sweepers were kept busy clearing away the piles of dung left by the horses.

In the countryside, buses were the cheapest and easiest way of getting about. In the cities, many buses had open-tops and were used on routes where there were no trams. Steam trains ran on the railways. In London, there were electric trains on the Underground.

A mobile sandwich service, 1927. Similar vehicles were used to sell ice-cream during the summer months.

Open-top buses fill the streets near the Bank of England, London, 1922.

Here are parts of one grandmother's memories of travel when she was young:

'All the trains had steam engines. If you looked out of the window when the train was moving you could get covered with black smuts.'

'We always travelled 3rd class. There were three classes in those days, 1st, 2nd and 3rd.'

'At some road junctions the tram had to stop so that the conductor could use a long pole to lift the arms from one set of overhead wires to another.'

Talk to old people about what travel was like when they were young. Make notes, or tape record what they say. Use libraries, local museums, transport museums and old family photos to research into trams, open-top buses, trolley buses and different classes of rail travel.

Traffic at London's Elephant and Castle, 1922. How many different forms of transport can you see in the picture? Notice the absence of traffic lights, pedestrian crossings, road markings and road signs.

6 The Steam Age

Most of the railway routes we use today are over 100 years old, and many date back to the 1830s or 1840s. The stations, bridges and other buildings have changed very little but the machinery and such things as the signalling equipment are more modern. Famous engineers, like Isambard Kingdom Brunel and Robert Stephenson, built the railways using the most up-to-date materials and ideas of their time. There are many fine examples of station roofs made of timber or cast-iron girders at Bristol, Edinburgh, Liverpool Street (London), and many smaller stations. Wrought-iron was used for the bridge across the Tamar in the West Country whereas the Forth Bridge,

Engineers such as Brunel and Stephenson were important figures in the development of the railway network. Brunel built many bridges, the last of which was the Royal Albert Bridge, at Saltash (shown in the picture). It was opened in 1858.

which was built later, used milled steel. The tunnels and viaducts, although less eye-catching, are also spectacular relics of the railway age.

When you travel by train try to imagine what life was like for the men who built the embankments and cuttings and laid the track. They were called 'navvies', a word first used for the men who built canals, once called inland navigations. The navvies moved from one camp to another as the line was built. They had to be very strong and tough because there was no machinery and the work was done with picks and shovels. They could move up to 400 wheelbarrows of soil each day and only used horses on the steep embankment sides.

Go to your public library and look through the collection of books in both the lending and reference sections. There will be several on the railways; look for those about the railways in your district. Imagine you were reporting the building of the railway near you for a local newspaper. Write an article about what you saw on a visit to the work in progress.

Above *A cartoon of a navvy, from* Punch *magazine, 1855.*

Below *Work in progress on the Tring cutting of the London and Birmingham railway, 1837.*

7 Travel on rails

Before the invention of the steam engine, coal and quarry-stone were carried over short distances along rails. At first, the heavy wagons ran along lengths of oak planks called 'trams' and these tracks became known as tramways. From about 1750 iron rails were used. These were called 'plates' and railway workers who lay rails are still called platelayers. By using iron wheels on the wagons and an iron tramway, it was possible for one horse to pull loads four times as heavy as it could pull along local roads. The iron rails were 'L' shaped which stopped the flat-rimmed wheels running off the track.

Many tramways were built to take coal to canals or minerals to iron works. The Peak Forest Tramway carried limestone and lead from mines in the hilly districts of Derbyshire to the canal serving Manchester. Like the canals, the tramways were built with as level a track as possible. Tunnels had to be cut and a special slope, called an incline, was made to link one level section with

A horse drawing a wagon-load of coal in eighteenth-century Newcastle. A horse on an iron tramway could pull a load four times as heavy as it could along a road.

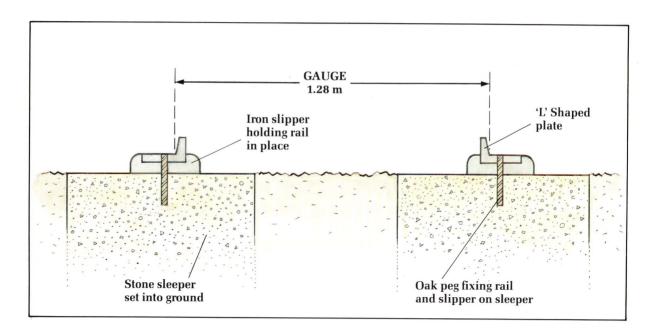

GAUGE
1.28 m

Iron slipper
holding rail
in place

'L' Shaped
plate

Stone sleeper
set into ground

Oak peg fixing rail
and slipper on sleeper

another. The wagons were pulled by horses but more power was needed to pull long trains of wagons. The first steam engines were made to provide this power. The routes of many tramways can still be followed, and the inclines, bridges, tunnels and stone sleeper blocks can be seen. Wagons and sections of the iron rails are preserved in museums such as the National Railway Museum at York.

Above *A cross-section of the track used on the Peak Forest Tramway (not to scale).*
Below *Horses harnessed to wagons of coal on the Derby Canal Tramroad. The tramroad ran from 1791–1908.*

8 Steamships

The first passenger steamship service was started by the *Comet* (invented by Henry Bell) on the River Clyde in 1812, thirteen years before the Stockton and Darlington Railway opened. The *Comet* steamed from Glasgow to Greenock at an average speed of 9 kph. In 1821 a steamship service was started between Dover and Calais, and four years later steamships started sailing from Newhaven to Dieppe. Steamships were more reliable than sailing ships on ferry routes. When the railways reached the cross-Channel ports in the 1840s it became possible to travel from London to Paris entirely by steampower. By the 1850s the Atlantic was regularly crossed by steamships and sailing vessels began to decline in importance.

The islands and west coast of Scotland were served by 'puffers', small steamships which carried food and essential goods. Puffers could be beached at high tide, unloaded at low tide and then refloated at the next high tide.

Above *Henry Bell's* Comet, *1812. The first steamboat to run commercially in Europe.*

Below *Brunel's streamship the* Great Eastern, *which could carry 4,000 passengers and sail non-stop from England to Australia. Another of Brunel's ships, the* Great Britain *was the first iron ship to cross the Atlantic.*

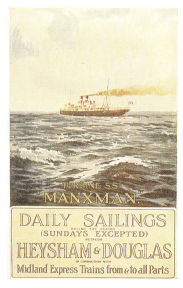

The early steamships were paddle steamers which made them slow. As a result, the engineer Brunel fitted the *Great Britain* with propellers, which were a great success. Paddle steamers were very popular as pleasure boats until the Second World War. In several parts of the country, such as on the River Clyde, Liverpool, North Wales and on the Thames estuary they were used to give holidaymakers boat trips. Some had a regular summer service, like the *Laguna Belle* which travelled between the pier at Clacton-on-Sea in Essex to London's Tower Pier. Only one paddle steamer, the *Waverley*, has survived and it is still used for pleasure trips on the Clyde.

Make a time chart like the one below for a ferry or pleasure boat service near you, or one you have used. The information you need can be found in books about ports or the boats.

Above left *The paddle steamer* Waverley *is still used to carry passengers on pleasure trips.* **Above right** *An advertisement for the steamship* Manxman, *travelling between the Isle of Man and Heysham in Lancashire. Posters, tickets and advertisements are useful sources of information.*

Newhaven as a cross-Channel port	
Date	**What happened**
1825	Steamer *Eclipse* started service to Dieppe.
1847	London-Newhaven railway opened.
1887	*Victoria* sank off Dieppe; 19 people drowned.
1891	First propeller-driven ferry, the *Seine*, started service.
1895	*Seaford* hit by *Lyon* in fog; sank without loss of life.
1930s	Steamers changed from burning coal to burning oil.
1939-45	No passenger service because of war.
1965	Car ferry service started.
1985	British passenger service ended; service continued by French boats.

9 The waterways

Is there a canal near you? What is it called? What use is made of it? Canals were built about two hundred years ago to carry manufactured goods, raw materials and minerals. At that time the Industrial Revolution was just beginning and the roads could not cope with the large loads going to and from the factories. The first canal was built in 1761 to carry coal from a mine to Manchester, a distance of 12 km. It halved the cost of coal in Manchester and made its owner, the Duke of Bridgewater, very rich. During the next sixty years canals were built in large numbers, mainly near the coalfields where industries and towns were growing fast.

There were no engines to power the canal boats so they were pulled by horses which walked along a specially-built towpath. Where the land was hilly, locks were built to act as water-steps between one level and another. A set of these

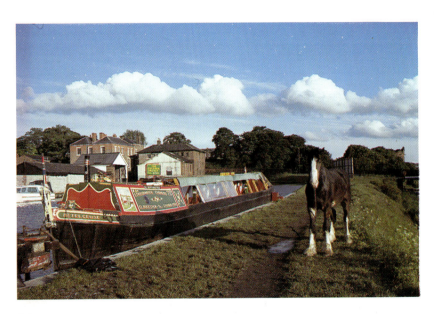

Lock workings

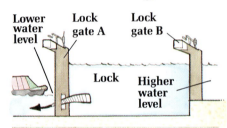

1. The boat needs to go up through the locks. The sluices on A are opened and the water level in the lock lowered.

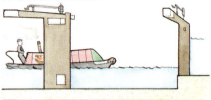

2. The boat moves into the lock and the gates are closed behind it.

3. The sluices on B are opened and the water level rises again.

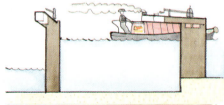

4. The gates in front of the boat are opened. The boat continues on its journey.

Above *How a canal lock works.*

A horse-drawn canal boat in the Chester Basin, Chester. Today, canals are used largely by holidaymakers.

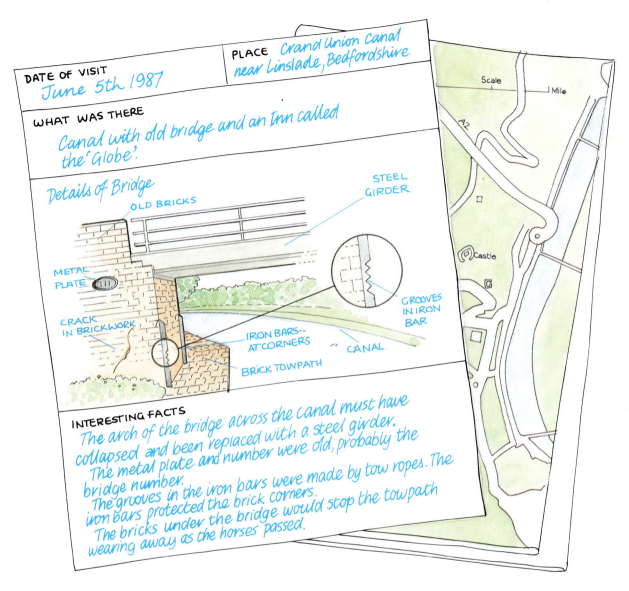

DATE OF VISIT
June 5th 1987

PLACE Grand Union Canal near Linslade, Bedfordshire

WHAT WAS THERE
Canal with old bridge and an Inn called the 'Globe'.

Details of Bridge

OLD BRICKS
STEEL GIRDER
METAL PLATE
CRACK IN BRICKWORK
IRON BARS AT CORNERS
BRICK TOWPATH
CANAL
GROOVES IN IRON BAR

INTERESTING FACTS
The arch of the bridge across the canal must have collapsed and been replaced with a steel girder.
The metal plate and number were old, probably the bridge number.
The grooves in the iron bars were made by tow ropes. The iron bars protected the brick corners.
The bricks under the bridge would stop the towpath wearing away as the horses passed.

Scale ___ Mile
A2
Castle

locks was called a staircase (as in Neptune's Staircase on the Caledonian Canal).

Factories and warehouses were built close to the canals, together with stables for the horses and pubs and shops for the people who lived and worked on the canal boats.

When the railways were built the canals lost most of their trade and were rarely used. With the spread of the railway network, some canals were filled in and railways were built along the course of the old canal. The first 25 km of the Aberdeen-Inverness railway are a good example.

When you visit canals, or other special transport sites, always make sure you go prepared, with pencil and paper, to record the most important details. The sheet above shows one useful way of going about this.

Today, some canals are busy once more, this time with pleasure boats. Conservation groups have repaired locks and cleared sections of canal choked with mud and weeds.

Choose a suitable spot on a canal where there are relics of the canal age. Make a chart like the one on page 25.

The boat people

In the early days of the canals, only the men worked on the boats and their families stayed on land. When the railways began to take trade away from the canals, the men's wages went down and it was cheaper for the whole family to live on the boat and help with the work. The boats were 21 m long and just over 2 m wide, with a small cabin at the rear about 3 m long. Boats were worked in pairs, with the wife steering the second boat, called the 'butty'. The children helped to work the locks, collect water and lead the horse in the days before engines were used. The family was

Above *A 'staircase' of locks, the Bingley Five Rise, on the Leeds to Liverpool Canal.*

Below *A narrow boat and its 'butty' on a canal near Watford, 1910. In the distance (left) you can see a horse helping to pull the boats along.*

always on the move so the children did not go to school regularly.

The boat was the only home the boat people had and they kept the small cabin clean and bright. A tradition grew up of decorating the cabins, especially the doors and objects they used such as buckets and pots. They painted castles and flowers in brilliant reds, greens and blues. The flowers they would have seen as they passed through the countryside, but no one is certain why they painted castles – perhaps it was because they hoped one day to live in one? Examples of the boat people's art can be seen at the Waterways Museum at Stoke Bruerne, Northamptonshire.

Mark out the size of a boat cabin in your bedroom. Why were the boats called 'narrow boats'? Paint a clay flower pot or a paper plate in the colours and style used by the boat people. Varnish your work when the paint is dry.

A christening on a narrow boat shortly after the death of Queen Victoria in 1901, hence the black clothes.

Below *These decorated pails, mugs and jugs are good examples of the boat people's art.*

10 Inland ports

Before the canals were built, rivers were used to carry goods which were difficult to transport on the poor roads. Heavy and bulky cargoes were also carried round the coast by sailing ships, which were small enough to sail up rivers to inland ports some distance from the sea. Today, it is very difficult for us to imagine some of the towns on small and narrow rivers as once being

Below *Sailing ships, known as collier brigs, were used to transport coal around the coast and up rivers to inland ports.*

ports. Places like Norwich, Chester, York, Lewes and Dumfries were inland ports with quays used by small sailing ships and barges. Large ships sailed round the coast carrying coal, timber and building stone. There was a regular trade in 'sea-coal' from the north-east coast to London and other ports in southern England.

Some inland ports on larger rivers, like Gainsborough on the river Trent and Worcester on the Severn, became more important when canals were dug linking them with the industrial areas of the Midlands.

All the inland ports declined when the railways took away their trade, but relics remain of their past. Place names such as Customs House Street, Pier Lane, Dock Road and the Ship Inn are useful clues to follow. There are also old wharfs, warehouses and factories as well as port records in local libraries.

The table below shows the number of people listed in local directories whose work was connected with the port of Gainsborough. Gainsborough became a railway town in 1841. Make a block graph to illustrate the changes shown in the table. Find out what each of the eight kinds of workers had to do.

Above *York was once a thriving inland port on the River Ouse.*

A seventeenth-century customs house.

Workers at Gainsborough connected with the port		
Kind of work	**1790**	**1844**
Sail and cloth makers	5	0
Rope makers	1	1
Shipwrights	1	1
Wharfingers	8	7
Agents for shipping companies	4	0
Navigation officers	1	0
Customs officers	1	0
Watermen	1	1

11 Sailing ships and ports

Cargoes and passengers were carried round the coast and overseas by sailing ships until steamships took their place about 100 years ago. Ports like Bristol, Liverpool, Glasgow and London were very busy trading centres in the eighteenth century. These ports were on river estuaries and could only be reached at high tides. At low tides the ships in port sat on the mud. This problem was solved by building docks into which the ships sailed at high tide. Gates held in the water and the ships remained afloat to unload.

Alongside these wet docks, as they were called, were built warehouses in which goods could be stored. These buildings were tall and made of brick or stone. Nearby there was usually a customs house, because duties had to be paid on goods such as tea and sugar. Many of these early docks, warehouses and other buildings are still there today. They are also to be found in smaller

Below left *Dockland buildings near London's Tower Bridge.*
Below right *St Katharine's Dock, London, is now a leisure area, and contains historic ships of varying kinds.*

ports such as Boston and Llanelli, or naval dockyards such as Portsmouth and Devonport.

Few of the sailing ships are left but paintings and models show what they looked like. One of the last clippers, the *Cutty Sark*, is open to visitors at Greenwich. Clippers were fast merchant ships which raced from the Far East or Australia. A cargo of tea or wool had a very high price if it reached the London market first. The *Cutty Sark* was the fastest sailing ship in the world. She sailed from Sydney to London in 1885 via the Cape of Good Hope in 9 weeks 4 days, a distance of approximately 28,000 km. Trace the route on a map or on a globe. How many kilometres did the *Cutty Sark* sail on average each day? How long does the journey take by air today?

Above *A clipper ship in full sail.*
Inset *The clipper* Cutty Sark *has been preserved and is open to the public at Greenwich, in London.*

12 The roads

Travel by stage coach

From about 1750, wealthy people travelled by stage coach unless they were rich enough to have their own coach and horses. They were called stage coaches because they stopped at regular stages to pick up and set down passengers or to change the horses. The most convenient stopping places were inns (known as coaching inns) along the main roads where meals and beds could be provided for the travellers and stables for the horses. Poor roads made travelling uncomfortable and slow, averaging less than 14 kph.

The most expensive seats were inside the coach with much lower fares for passengers sitting outside with the coachman. In 1812 three passengers sitting outside from Bath to Chippenham froze to death and there are many accounts of coaches

The mail coach on the Bath to London run, 1830. The mail is collected from the postmaster (still wearing his nightcap!).

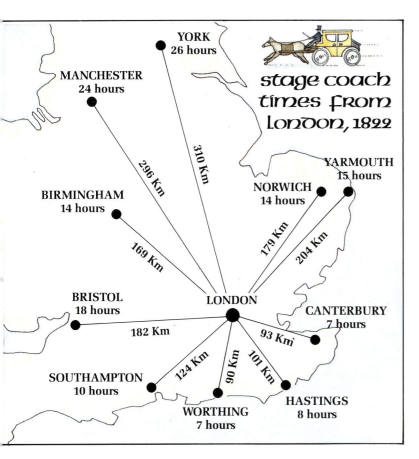

stage coach times from London, 1822

YORK
26 hours

MANCHESTER
24 hours

310 Km

296 Km

BIRMINGHAM
14 hours

169 Km

YARMOUTH
15 hours

NORWICH
14 hours

179 Km

204 Km

BRISTOL
18 hours

182 Km

LONDON

CANTERBURY
7 hours

93 Km

124 Km

90 Km

101 Km

SOUTHAMPTON
10 hours

WORTHING
7 hours

HASTINGS
8 hours

Above *A masked highwayman, armed with a pistol, demands money and valuables from the passengers of a stage coach. Find out about one highwayman, such as Dick Turpin. Design a poster offering a reward leading to the capture of the highwayman.*

Above left *Compare these times for stage coach journeys in 1822 with the times it would take today to complete the same trips by coach or train.*

turning over. Other dangers included the risk of being held up by highwaymen or the coachman getting drunk at one of the stages.

In the 1820s the main roads were busy with stage coaches, smaller private carriages and mail coaches. The mail coaches had red wheels and black side-panels and carried a few passengers as well as mail. An armed guard travelled on the coach sounding a horn to warn other travellers to get out of the way. By 1840, the coach services were coming to an end because the railways were spreading across the country.

Use the distances and times on the diagram above to work out the average speed of coaches going to York, Yarmouth and Bristol. With the help of rail or coach timetables draw a similar diagram showing the times taken today.

The Turnpikes

Have you ever been in a car when the driver has had to pay to use the road, cross a bridge or drive through a tunnel? In the eighteenth century the poor quality of the roads hindered industries and trade. To encourage improvements, Parliament allowed private companies to charge a sum of money, called a toll, on vehicles or farm animals using a certain section of a road. The money collected was spent on improving and repairing roads and bridges. The companies were called Turnpike Trusts.

The name 'turnpike' came from the gates placed across the road. They were often fitted with spikes to prevent horseriders jumping over to avoid paying the toll. Near the gate was a cottage for the gate-keeper, known as a tollhouse. On some roads there were a great many tollhouses. Between London and Worthing, a distance of 90 km, there were 14 tollgates. Travellers had to stop at each one, but where the same Turnpike Trust owned several gates, only one ticket had to be paid for. Some people tried to avoid paying the toll by riding their carriages or driving their animals across nearby fields. Turnpikes were not popular, but the state of the roads was improved.

In Scotland the Jacobite rising of highland families in 1715 frightened the government in London. General Wade was ordered to build new roads and bridges so that troops could be moved into the highlands quickly. These roads and bridges were strongly built and are still used today, the most famous bridge being that which crosses the Tay at Aberfeldy. The picture opposite shows some things to look for when travelling by road (mounting blocks helped riders to get on their horses; spur stones protected the corners of buildings from damage by vehicles).

Above *The Tyburn Turnpike (Marble Arch) in London, 1813, showing the tollhouse and a toll being collected from the horseman near the gatepost.*

Opposite *Some items to look out for when you travel by road.*

Below *This milestone shows the distance to Bow Bells Church in London. It could be understood by travellers who could not read.*

at the Roadside

Tollhouse

Horse trough

Mounting block

Bollard

Cobblestones

Tethering post

Coaching inn

Spur stone

Roads in the Middle Ages

When the Normans conquered England in 1066, the best roads were those that had been built by the Romans a thousand years earlier. They were badly in need of repair and travel was slow and uncomfortable. Along these routes and trackways passed merchants, pedlars, officials, soldiers and villagers travelling to market. Pilgrims could also be seen making their way to shrines like the tomb of St Thomas à Becket at Canterbury. The route they used became known as the Pilgrim's Way. Travellers could stay at monasteries or hostels owned by the monks.

Below *Pilgrims on their way to the shrine of St Thomas à Becket, at Canterbury Cathedral.*

Inset *The murder of Becket in 1170, by knights of King Henry II.*

Many of our winding roads are the result of medieval routeways following dry ground and keeping to field boundaries. Where they crossed rivers, bridges were built. Some of these old bridges made of stone can still be seen. They often had recesses along them where people on foot could stand to allow horses and carriages to pass. In towns, the streets were narrow and often surfaced with cobblestones. Today some of these streets have been turned into precincts and closed to traffic.

During the sixteenth century, trade grew and the increase in traffic cut up the soft surface of the roads. A law was passed making each parish responsible for the roads running through it. The villagers had to work on the roads for four days each year. Later, a tax on property, called a rate, helped to pay for highway repairs. However, travellers continued to tell grim stories about the state of the roads.

Imagine you were on a pilgrimage in the Middle Ages, write your diary for one day's travel.

This medieval bridge in Sussex has recesses along each side, where people could stand to allow horses and carriages to pass by.

clues to Roman Roads
What to look for

1. Place names such as Street, Stratford, Stan, Stone, Streat.
Places with these words as part of their name may be near a Roman Road.

2. A straight modern road which suddenly winds, the straight line continuing as a lane, track or line of hedges.

ROMAN ROAD
(course of)

4. Marked on Ordnance Survey maps 1:50 000 and 1:25 000

3. A straight road that winds for a short distance and then straightens along its old course.

Special note: Not all straight roads are Roman roads, check your discovery on a map.

Roman Roads

When the Romans invaded Britain in 43 BC they found a network of earth roads which were little used. These roads kept to the hills and avoided swampy areas where possible. The Romans wanted to move troops and supplies long distances and planned roads to link military or trading posts by the quickest and easiest routes. As well as building new roads, they also extended and improved the existing road system. Many of their roads centred on London but there were also important cross-country routes such as Watling Street, from Chester to York. The roads were built as straight as possible, but in hilly districts or at river crossings, bends were sometimes necessary. They used local materials to form a surface. If there was no stone nearby, gravel, cobbles or sand were used instead. The roads were usually between 5 m and 8 m wide so that carts and chariots could pass one another. They were built on an embankment called an agger. The surface was ridged and the water ran off into ditches.

Below *This modern road follows the same course as part of the old Roman road known as Stane Street.*

Above *A Roman carriage with passengers. In Roman times – and for many centuries after – people could only travel by foot, on horseback or by horse-drawn carriage.*

Just as motorways have service stations, so the Romans built posting stations. These were approximately 20 km apart, the distance a soldier could march in one day carrying all his equipment. At these posting stations the soldiers could have a bath, rest and groom their horses.

The original surfaces of the main Roman roads have been buried beneath modern roads but there are still sections of roads to be discovered in the countryside where lanes and tracks follow the routes the roads once took. Copy the cross-section below and underneath draw a scale cross-section of a motorway or dual carriageway.

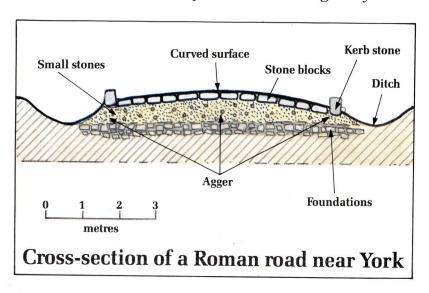

Cross-section of a Roman road near York

13 A transport project

There are lots of clues and suggestions in this book that will help you to discover more about transport in your district. Now is the time to plan a project in which you can explore your district and collect interesting material. First you must choose a topic. This is not as easy as it sounds. It is no good choosing a subject which has no links with your area. For example, if you live in Birmingham there should be plenty of information about local canals in the libraries, but little on coastal ports. Never be too ambitious – always choose a topic which is very limited. For example, you might choose as your topic, 'The Kennet and Avon Canal at Devizes', 'Dundee Harbour', or 'A Local Railway Engine Driver's Life in the 1930s'. You may want to choose a more general topic using local information whenever possible: for example, 'Bicycles in the Past'.

In researching a project on bicycles, you may come across many unusual examples. **Below left** *Johnson's Pedestrian Hobby-horse, 1819. The rider sat astride the machine on a saddle and used his legs to push himself along.*

Below right *A penny farthing bicycle of 1896 – can you imagine how difficult it would have been to balance on a bicycle like this?*

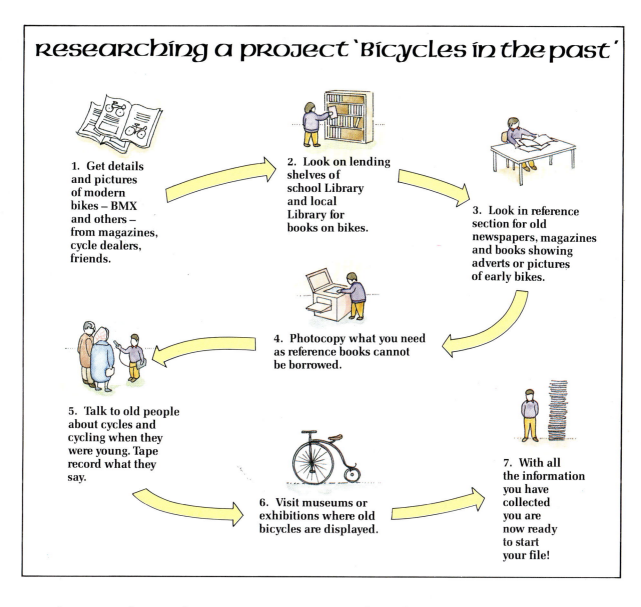

researching a project 'Bicycles in the past'

1. Get details and pictures of modern bikes – BMX and others – from magazines, cycle dealers, friends.

2. Look on lending shelves of school Library and local Library for books on bikes.

3. Look in reference section for old newspapers, magazines and books showing adverts or pictures of early bikes.

4. Photocopy what you need as reference books cannot be borrowed.

5. Talk to old people about cycles and cycling when they were young. Tape record what they say.

6. Visit museums or exhibitions where old bicycles are displayed.

7. With all the information you have collected you are now ready to start your file!

When you have chosen a topic get together the essential equipment. You will need a clipboard, paper, pencils and some 5p and 10p coins for photocopiers. You may also find a camera, tape recorder and measuring tape useful. Before you start, decide how the material you collect will be presented. Putting your work in a loose-leaf file has many advantages, as pages can be added or taken out, and illustrations mounted on separate sheets.

The diagram above shows the various stages in

The diagram above will help you to organize your project.

collecting material for the project 'Bicycles in the Past'. Other topics might start differently; for example, a project on a local canal would probably start with an outside visit, the library research coming later.

Writing and presenting your project

Nobody wants to read a project which is untidy, poorly arranged or dull. It needs to look attractive and to contain plenty of interesting photos, sketches, charts and diagrams. When you have collected all your material, follow this plan:

1. Decide how the topic should be divided up into sections or chapters. For example, the 'Bicycles in the Past' project might start with a section on 'The First Bicycles', followed by one on 'The Penny Farthing', and so on. The project might end with a section on modern bikes.

2. Sort your notes and illustrations into piles,

Below left *'Cornering' during the Errand Boy's Annual Derby, Maidstone, 1935. Your research into local transport may reveal some unusual facts or events, such as this race which was held every year for local delivery boys.*

Below right *The author's aunt, with her first bicycle in 1910. To stop clothes getting dirty or tangled up, the chain was hidden inside a metal case.*

one for each section. If one section does not seem to have enough material, find some more or combine it with another section.

3. Mount your photographs, draw good copies of sketches you made on visits and prepare charts and diagrams. Remember that each illustration will need a title and some writing underneath describing what it shows. Add captions and labels whenever possible, like those added to the advertisement below.

4. Write the chapters one at a time with the illustrations in front of you. Do not copy long sections from books – use your own words. Any quotations you include should be in speech marks.

5. Finally, put your pages together in a file, number them and add a title page. Now you have a piece of your own research to be proud of!

An advertisement for bicycles in Gowland's Eastbourne Directory *of 1892. When you illustrate your project, remember to add captions, labels and headings to your pictures to make them as informative as possible.*

Solid tyre   No mudguard   Metal front brake   Bracket for lamp   No gears   High seat with springs   No back brake

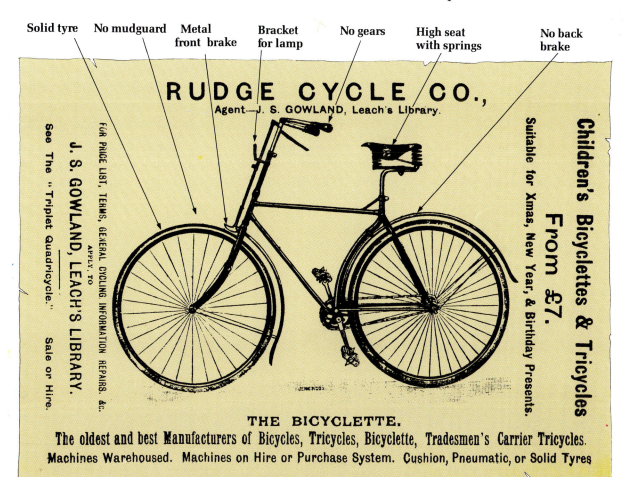

RUDGE CYCLE CO.,
Agent—J. S. GOWLAND, Leach's Library.

See The "Triplet Quadricycle."   J. S. GOWLAND, LEACH'S LIBRARY.   Sale or Hire.

FOR PRICE LIST, TERMS, GENERAL CYCLING INFORMATION REPAIRS, &c. APPLY TO

Suitable for Xmas, New Year, & Birthday Presents.   Children's Bicyclettes & Tricycles From £7.

JENKINSON.

THE BICYCLETTE.
The oldest and best Manufacturers of Bicycles, Tricycles, Bicyclette, Tradesmen's Carrier Tricycles. Machines Warehoused. Machines on Hire or Purchase System. Cushion, Pneumatic, or Solid Tyres.

Places to visit

Books, newspapers and magazines in your local libraries should give you a great deal of material about transport. In addition, many museums have sections containing transport exhibits. There are also specialist museums which are well worth visiting. You will probably want to add more names and addresses to this selection:

England
Exeter Maritime Museum, Devon – ships and naval equipment.
Great Western Railway Museum, Swindon, Wiltshire – steam engines; railway equipment; restored workers' cottages.
Ironbridge Gorge Museum, Ironbridge, Shropshire – cast iron rails; Shropshire Canal.
Midland Motor Museum, Bridgnorth, Staffordshire – sports cars; racing cycles.
Monkwearmouth Station Museum, Sunderland, Tyne and Wear – Victorian station; railway relics.
National Maritime Museum, Greenwich, London – model ships; navigation instruments.
National Motor Museum, Beaulieu, Hampshire – vehicles of all ages.
National Railway Museum, York – steam engines; railway equipment.
North of England Open Air Museum, Beamish, Co. Durham – steam engines; railway track.
Railways Museum, Stoneygate, Leicestershire – railway equipment.
S. S. Great Britain, Bristol, Avon – Brunel's restored first steamship.
Waterways Museum, Stoke Bruerne, Northants – canal equipment.

Scotland
Doune Motor Museum, Doune, Perthshire – vintage cars.
Grampian Transport Museum, Alford, Aberdeenshire.
Museum of Transport, Glasgow – all types of vehicles.
Royal Scottish Museum, Edinburgh – aeronautical relics.

Wales
National Museum of Wales, Cardiff – tramways; maritime exhibits.
Welsh Folk Museum, Cardiff – tollhouse.

Above *Newspapers, both local and national, can provide us with a wealth of information on transport in the past.*

Further reading

Booth, Gavin, *Buses* (Wayland, 1982)
Case, S. L., *Inland Transport* (Evans, 1979)
Cockett, Mary, *Roads and Travelling* (Blackwell, 1964)
Cosson, Neil, *The BP Book of Industrial Archaeology* (David & Charles, 1975)

Embleton, G. A., *Passenger Aircraft* (Wayland, 1982)

Gregory, S., *Railways and Life in Britain* (Ginn and Co., 1969)

Hammersley, A., *Roads and Road Transport* (Blandford, 1970)

Hammersley, A. and Perry, G., *Railways and Rail Transport* (Blandford, 1971)

Hennessey, R. A. S., *Transport* (Batsford, 1966)

Metcalfe, L., *Bridges and Bridgebuilding* (Blandford, 1970)

Posthumus, Cyril, *Cars* (Wayland, 1982)

Vialls, C., *Canals* (A&C Black, 1975)

Vialls, C., *Roads* (A&C Black, 1971)

A travel time chart, outlining the major changes in the history of transport in Britain. Make your own chart, adding more dates and events – perhaps even your ideas of how transport will develop in the future.

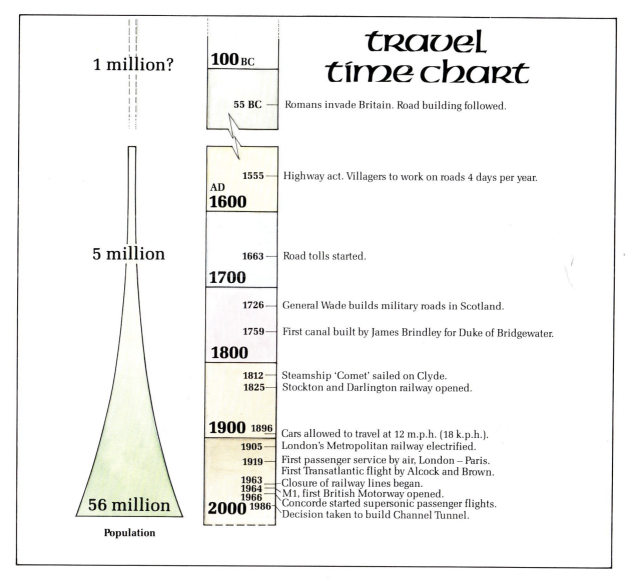

travel time chart

1 million?

100 BC

55 BC — Romans invade Britain. Road building followed.

1555 — Highway act. Villagers to work on roads 4 days per year.

AD **1600**

5 million

1663 — Road tolls started.

1700

1726 — General Wade builds military roads in Scotland.

1759 — First canal built by James Brindley for Duke of Bridgewater.

1800

1812 — Steamship 'Comet' sailed on Clyde.
1825 — Stockton and Darlington railway opened.

1900 1896 — Cars allowed to travel at 12 m.p.h. (18 k.p.h.).
1905 — London's Metropolitan railway electrified.
1919 — First passenger service by air, London – Paris.
First Transatlantic flight by Alcock and Brown.
1963 — Closure of railway lines began.
1964 — M1, first British Motorway opened.
1966
2000 1986 — Concorde started supersonic passenger flights.
Decision taken to build Channel Tunnel.

56 million

Population

Glossary

Agger The raised ridge of earth on which a Roman road was usually built. It gave the road good drainage, the water running off into ditches on either side.

Boat people The families who lived and worked on the canal boats. They had their own traditions and way of life.

By-pass A road which is made round a built-up area to allow traffic to avoid congestion inside a town.

Canal lock A section of canal with concrete or stone sides and gates at either end, which can be used to raise or lower a boat from one level to another.

Cat's-eyes Glass reflectors set into the road to indicate traffic lanes at night.

Clipper A fast sailing ship designed for carrying cargoes of tea, wool or other goods from Asia or Australia.

Control tower The tower at an airport from which aircraft taking off and landing receive their instructions.

Cutting An opening made through a ridge of ground to make a level, or nearly level routeway. Cuttings can be found along railway lines, canals and some roads.

Duties Taxes paid on goods.

Embankment An artificial ridge of ground made to provide a level, or fairly level routeway. Embankments can be found along railway lines, canals and some roads.

Fly-over A road built on concrete pillars which goes over another road so that the two sets of traffic are separated and do not converge at a road junction.

Hovercraft A vehicle which rides on a cushion of air and uses propellers for movement. Hovercraft are mainly used for crossing water.

Incline A specially-built slope used to raise or lower wagons on tramways from one level to another.

Industrial Revolution The period after about 1760 when steam power and the invention of different types of machinery resulted in Britain becoming the leading industrial country in the world. It brought about major changes in where and how people lived, with a shift of population from the countryside to towns and cities.

Narrow boat A boat designed for use on the canals. It was just over 20 m long but only about 2 m wide.

Package tour A holiday trip arranged by a tour operator which usually includes travel and accommodation.

Paddle steamer A boat with a steam engine which drove large iron paddles set on either side of the hull.

Penny Farthing One of the early bicycles that had a very large front wheel and a very small rear wheel. The wheels reminded people of the coins of the time (the large penny piece and the small farthing).

Platelayer A person employed on railways to lay and maintain the track.

Posting station A Roman centre surrounded by a wall and built beside a main road. It was used by travellers and troops who could wash, eat and rest there.

Precinct An area in a town where traffic is not permitted. Streets are made into precincts so that shoppers and other people can walk about in a traffic-free area.

Ring road A circular road built round a city and connected to roads coming into the city. Traffic can avoid congestion in a city by using a ring road. The M25 around London is a good example.

Sea-coal Coal carried by sea, usually from the Durham or Northumberland coasts to London and the towns of southern England

Stage coach A coach pulled by horses which ran a regular service for passengers over a certain route. It stopped along the route at 'stages' where horses were changed and passengers could eat and rest.

Tarmacadam A road surface formed by using stone chips coated in tar.

Tollhouse The cottage built beside a tollgate where the gate keeper lived.

Turnpike Trust A private company that was set up with responsibility for the upkeep of a stretch of road. Money to carry out maintenance and improvements was raised by charging travellers a toll.

Veteran car Any car made before 1919. The true veteran cars were those made before 1905.

Viaduct A long bridge made of brick or stone built to carry a road or railway across a valley or dip in the ground.

Wet dock A dock with lock gates which allows a ship to remain afloat whatever the state of the tide.

Wharf A wooden or stone platform beside which a ship may be moored for loading or unloading.

Index

Picture Acknowledgements
The publishers would like to thank the following for supplying pictures: BBC Hulton 8 (left), 16 (top and bottom), 17; Beken of Cowes 23 (top left); Gavin Booth 5; Bridgeman Art Library 33 (right); British Waterways Board 24 (bottom), 26 (bottom), 27 (top and bottom), 44; Mary Evans 12 (bottom), 13, 22, 23 (top right), 40 (right); Michael Holford 22 (top); Hutchison 6 (bottom), 7 (bottom), 19, 29 (top); Cliff Lines 34 (bottom), 37, 38 (bottom), 42 (right); Archie Miles 14 (top and bottom), 30 (left); National Maritime Museum 28; National Railway Museum 21 (bottom); Ann Ronan 18, 19 (top and bottom), 13, 23 (top right), 40 (left); Ronald Sheridan 36 (inset), 39 (top); TOPHAM 4, 8 (right), 30 (right), 31 (inset), 42; Zefa 7 (top), 11 (top), 12 (top), 15 (top). All artwork is by Stephen Wheele, except 36 (John James). The remaining pictures are from the Wayland Picture Library.